SWEET REVENGE

SWEET REVENGE

Irene Isoken Salami-Agunloye

Africa World Press, Inc.

P.O. Box 1892
Trenton, NJ 08607

P.O. Box 48
Asmara, ERITREA

Africa World Press, Inc.

P.O. Box 1892
Trenton, NJ 08607

P.O. Box 48
Asmara, ERITREA

Book Design: Aliya Books
Cover Design: Dapo Ojo-Ade

Library of Congress Cataloging-in-Publication Data

Salami-Agunloye, Irene Isoken.
 Sweet revenge / by Irene Isoken Salami-Agunloye.
     p. cm.
  ISBN 1-59221-456-8 -- ISBN 1-59221-457-6 (pbk.)
  1. Women--Nigeria--Drama. I. Title.
  PR9387.9.S218S94 2007
  822'.92--dc22

                                    2007015970

CHARACTERS

Aisosa	Sota's Nigerian wife
Sota	Aisosa's husband
Cheryl	Sota's British wife
Regie	Sota's friend
Ede	Aisosa's friend & Nosa's wife
Nosa	Ede's husband and Sota's friend
Isi	Nanny
Ota	Aisosa and Sota's Son
Madam Power-Power	Female political leader
Madam Show Dem	Female politician
Madam Speaker	Female politician
Madam Executive	Female politician
Abdul	Personal Assistant to Aisosa
Aboki	Gateman
Women politicians	

MOVEMENT 1

[This scene takes place in London. Sota is seen in front of his computer reading an e-mail, which he eventually prints.]

Sota: O my God, what? Return home! Return home to what? To politics? Am I a politician? What do I know about politics apart from what we were doing in the Movement for Democracy here? I have been away from home for eight years now. Eight years! Eight good years. How time flies. From a four-year study-leave for a PhD in International Relations, to being trapped in this country. I remember telling my wife Aisosa when I left, "You stay back to take care of our children while I go in search of the Golden Fleece." Like a dutiful wife, she obeyed. She has faithfully waited for my return all these years. I have fabricated tales after tales each day to explain my prolonged stay here in England. Now I have taken up a job and settled down comfortably in London. Comfortably, yes comfortably. And here comes this mail, saying "return home immediately." This is beyond me. Return home? At this time? What will I tell Aisosa? Yet their call is so strong, return home they press. What am I to do? My people have called and no doubt, I must respond to it. They say, "Your time has come. Now is your time to lead our people out of the clutches of the oppressors."

[He reads the mail further]

"The Senatorial seat has been zoned to our local government. You are our best choice for this position, the best suited for it. You have always written to us about the need for good governance, you fought for it from over there; now return home to establish these ideals. Please return home, return home to us immediately. You belong here."

[He reads the last words nearly inaudibly; bows his head in deep thought, and then lifts it up slowly]

The drums beat, they roll out rhythmical beats, inviting me home, I cannot turn down their offer, I must respond. I must step out and match its rhythm, I cannot fail my people. No, I will not turn down their invitation. They have reposed their confidence in me and I will not fail them. I cannot let them down. Together we will transform our land.

[Light out]

4

MOVEMENT 2

[Sota's study. He is working on the computer. He is moody and looking very confused. He talks to himself occasionally in whispers, picks up his phone.]

Sota: Hello, ... yes, hello... Oh I see, please tell him to call when he returns.

[Returns to his computer]

How one's life can change overnight. This indeed is a big challenge. I think this will do.

[Going through the mail he has typed on the computer]

[Enter Cheryl]

Cheryl: Sota, why this long face? You have been putting up this act since yesterday. Is anything the matter?

Sota: Not really.

Cheryl: What do you mean by "not really"?

Sota: Well, it's just that my people have invited me to come home and represent them in the country's National Assembly as a senator.

Cheryl: What? Invited you home to contest for a political position? You are returning to your

	country and you think that is not a big issue?
Sota:	It is not an issue.
Cheryl:	Yes, for you it isn't. But for me it is a real big issue. Our coming together was based on the fact that you promised never to return to your country but to make Britain your home.
Sota:	Honey, I have not changed my mind about that at all. We will still keep our home here. The senatorial position is at least a four-year-tenure, but can extend to eight years or more if they desire.
Cheryl:	Yes, eight short years. Time flies you know. You think I will be here waiting for you?
	[Sarcastically]
	Very, very funny.
	[Laughs]
Sota:	*[Moves over to Cheryl]*
	Cheryl, there is no cause for alarm. Things will work out well.
Cheryl:	Yes, just fine indeed. I wish this had happened seven months ago.
Sota:	What do you mean?
Cheryl:	*[Rising]*
	Of course you know exactly what I mean.
Sota:	Why are you making things so difficult for me, Cheryl? I promise you, nothing will change.

[Holding her reassuringly]

Cheryl: Yes, nothing will change. You will drive over here every weekend. After all, Africa is a few miles from London, isn't it?

Sota: Don't be sarcastic. We are serious here.

Cheryl: I quite agree with you. Sota, you insisted I should have this baby.

Sota: Yes I did. Am I denying that?

Cheryl: Then you have to stay back till the baby is born before you disappear to Africa.

Sota: Nigeria, you mean?

Cheryl: Whatever.

Sota: Cheryl, you have to understand Nigerian politics. In some instances, people from our locality invite us to represent them. This is politics of window of opportunity. If this opportunity is not utilised, it closes up and may not open up again. This opening is an honourable gesture. With such honour bestowed on one, you have no choice but to respond positively by not turning down the people's request. Cheryl, you see I have no choice in this matter. This is beyond me. It is difficult to refuse this invitation and offer. Refusing this request will alienate my children and me from my people and community forever. Remember, how hard we in the Movement for Democracy back here fought for our country's return to democracy?

Cheryl: What has that got to do with being here when the baby is born? This is all about priority.

Sota: Please honey, be more understanding. This indeed is a golden opportunity that I must not miss. You see, for years we asked the soldiers to leave. 'Away soldier boys!!' 'Away to the barracks where you belong!!' The people of my country campaigned for over thirty years for their removal, now they have packed their bags and baggage and departed as we demanded and we are now faced with the challenge of putting our house in order. Putting things right after so many years of damage is an enormous task, Cheryl.

[There is a knock on the door]

Sota: Yes, come in. I sure need some assistance right now.

[Enter Regie, dressed in formal Nigerian attire]

Cheryl: Hi Reji.

Sota: Honey, how many times will I correct you? It's not Reji but Regie, the short form of Omoregie.

Regie: That's alright. She can call me whatever she is comfortable with.

Cheryl: Thanks, Reji. I can see you are all dressed up for a big occasion.

Regie: You are correct. The Movement for Democracy is meeting to nominate delegates who will travel home to monitor the forthcoming elections in Nigeria. Sota is not attending because he is a candidate.

Cheryl: Oh really? You mean it's such a big thing?

Sota: What do you mean? Of course it is. No country's elections are trivial issues. No matter how insignificant that country is in the eyes of other nations.

Cheryl: O, pardon my ignorance then.

Regie: I heard that our people have invited you to come and vie for the forthcoming elections.

Sota: Imagine that, it came as a shock to me.

Regie: A good shock I must say. What better reward can there be than to fight and be asked to partake of the booties of the war? What can be better than fighting for the liberation of your country from militocracy, only to be called upon to establish democracy? It is an honour Sota, it really is. You can't refuse it. Accept it Sota for the sake of our country...!

Cheryl: Just like that?

Regie: Yes Cheryl, you see sometimes, even when our country does not deserve it, we must make sacrifices for her. The Whitman's land is good, but home is where we all belong, not here. Sota, you have come; you have achieved, but please retrace your steps home. Return home and help transform your land. Go teach our people the essence of good governance. They really do need it.

Cheryl: Reji, you speak so passionately about Africa, you must love Africa very much.

Regie: Nigeria? O yes! I love my country and my continent. Cheryl you need to know the amount of wealth God has invested in Nigeria. It is enough to enrich the entire sub-Saharan Africa. Harnessing it for the benefit of all has been our major challenge.

Cheryl: Really? Sounds interesting.

Sota: So, Cheryl, you see why I am so confused. I feel bad turning my back on all I have achieved here. I have no choice though.

Regie: O, yes, you don't. Sota, accepting our people's call to return home is a bold step; it will do us proud.

Cheryl: Your country must be lucky to have people like you.

Regie: We have no choice, Cheryl, it's the only country we can call our own. At each stage we've had to fight for our liberation, liberation from colonial power and liberation from the repressive military regime; which always came as redeemer but once in power we always needed to be redeemed from them. They claim to be there to salvage the situation from oppressive politicians but each time they came, they held on tightly to power, refusing to relinquish it. This last time, Cheryl, things became so bad, they held on to power, held the people hostage for a long time until the Movement for Democracy mobilized and attracted international attention. As external pressure matched the internal pressure, they had no choice but to leave the stage.

Cheryl: Without any bloodshed?

Regie: Well, without major casualties. God has been generous to our nation. The change we dreamt of is here.

Cheryl: No wonder the military held unto power for so long. No one was ready to pay the price for the liberty and the change you wanted.

Regie: People did pay. But you must understand that there is little people can do when confronted with guns ready to fire. The military instilled fear in us; they hijacked our power, controlled our destiny and dictated our pace of development.

Sota: Don't forget the crowd renting. They rented crowd to march in support of their continued leadership. Bootlickers, profiteers of the oligarchy, acted as cheerleaders spurring them on.

Regie: They easily became obsessed with power

Sota: Yes, they found power too delicious that they were reluctant to let go.

Regie: In the very few attempts at civil rule, before the politicians even opened the door to their offices, marshal music rented the still morning air and of course the usual refrain of croaking voice dragged the country decades back.

           [Collects a cap that resembles an army cap and adorns his head with it, sits on a nearby chair with a table. He rolls up newspaper, which he uses as a microphone]

           Fellow countrymen, we have observed with great shock the gross mismanagement of our national resources by irresponsible politi-

cians. Although we are reluctant to inter-
fere, we cannot stay back in the barracks
and watch our country being plundered and
destroyed wantonly. We have sworn to de-
fend the unity, integrity, honour and glory
of our nation and that we will do without
fear or favour. We are here for a brief period
to correct the situation; we will return to
the barracks as soon as we clean up the mess.
There shall be no sacred cows. The consti-
tution is hereby suspended. The former
president has been dismissed with immediate effect. All ministers are dismissed with
immediate effect. All governors, local government chairmen are to remain under
house arrest until further notice. The military government will set up a political tran-
sition and a restoration committee in due
course. A new election timetable will be an-
nounced very soon. This government will
not tolerate any indiscipline. Fellow Nigeri-
ans, a dusk to dawn curfew is now in place.
You are to go about your business as law-
abiding citizens. Long live Federal Republic
of Nigeria.

*[Steps out of character, Sota embrace him and
they both begin to laugh]*

Cheryl: This is horrendous. What efforts did people
           at home make to regain power from them?

Regie: Well, apart from our efforts here, some el-
           ders initiated talks towards the end.

Cheryl: Talks? Just talks? Of what use was that when
           your house was already on fire. Where were
           your mighty men of valour?

Regie:	Hiding in their closets. It became too dangerous for the men to do more than what they did. They supported the women anyway.
Cheryl:	And the women? What about the women?
Regie:	Oh! Our dear mothers, they put in all they could. They held rallies, pleaded with the wives of military leaders, led protests marches; infact one woman who strongly opposed them was shot dead one early morning. She paid dearly with her life.

[Women protesting, singing and carrying placards, holding press conferences is projected on the screen at backstage. The killing of the woman is shown. A lady making a press statement is also seen]

Cheryl:	And the men?
Regie:	I said hiding in their closets. When they dared to come out they wore badges, badges that identified them with the military government.
Cheryl:	Now, I see why you are so excited about the dawn of this new Nigeria.
Sato:	Cheryl, you are damn right. That is why I must go home to answer the call of my people to recreate and build up this new Nigeria so that Nigeria can stand tall among the super powers of the world.
Cheryl:	And what role will the women play in this new Nigeria?
Sota:	Relax, don't be too fast, Cheryl. We have just commenced. All that will be worked out later. As soon as things are sorted out, they

will be duly compensated.

Cheryl: Did I hear you say "compensated"?

Sota: Yes, what about that?

Cheryl: You talk as if they are not part of the system. They should be involved right from the start.

Sota: Well, things don't work that way in Africa. We take a lot of things into consideration.

Regie: That is why you are going there. Sota, you are going there to join others to change things. Change attitudes, change values positively. You are going for change, Sota.

[Stands up]

Excuse me, I want to make a call outside.

[Exits]

Sota: Changes don't happen so fast. There are other things we must consider

Cheryl: Like what?

Sota: Many things that you may not understand. In any case we have promised to compensate them.

Cheryl: What do you mean by that? Nothing concrete beyond promises you mean? I thought you said that men and women fought for your country's return to democracy, so why sideline the women?

Sota: I really can't say much. I am out here and can't speak for my country because I do not know the details.

[Enters Regie]

Cheryl:	It seems your country is made up of only men; women are nowhere in your national agenda. They are at the margin, nowhere near the centre. Good luck to you all.
Regie:	Things are not really that bad, Cheryl, but Sota you need to champion the fight against the attitude of shutting women out. As a nation we must constantly be conscious of the fact that Nigeria is made up of men and women. Mainstreaming women into governance is a task we must all carry out at any cost.
Sota:	Well, I can't say much on this side of the world. When I arrive in Nigeria, I will see what the situation is and then work out how women can be integrated into the system.
Regie:	And what if the situation is not favourable?
Sota:	Then there is nothing I can do.
Cheryl:	Nothing you can do? Both of you have just related how with determination you were able to bring about a major change in your country; you fought for it and got it. Why can't you fight for equal participation too? Fight for it and you will remain a hero forever.
Sota:	Not in Nigeria, you will be called "woman wrapper."
Regie:	So what, Sota, so what? When we laboured for the birth of the new Nigeria, were we not called names? We were unpopular. Did we not sacrifice our time, money, and life so

that Nigeria would come alive again? Sota, you have a new task, fight for the women, fight with them to realise their dreams.

Cheryl: I am very sure African women can fight their own battles. From all I have heard, they are equal to the task.

Regie: Certainly, you are right, but you see, Cheryl, in Africa, men and women are meant to support one another even though most of the time this is not the case.

Cheryl: How sad. Sota, if your vision is sincere, here is a task for you.

Sota: Well, I can't make any commitment.

Regie: Sota, if you know that you can't make sacrifices, better remain here. If you go with this attitude you may become a stumbling block or a clog in the wheel of their progress. Your action denotes lack of heroic will.

Cheryl: I think I agree with you, Reji. Better stay back than make a mess of the situation.

Sota: Yes, of course, I will stay back and do as you wish.

Cheryl: Honey, don't get me wrong I love Nigeria. I feel the pain of the Nigerian women. Sota, you are not as compassionate about them as Regie is. You can imagine what it is like to be excluded from a system that belongs to all. Being marginalised is dehumanising.

Regie: Sota, remember the ideals we fought for: dignity, unity and honour for all, a new Nigeria, where no one is oppressed.

Cheryl:	Yes and the labours of your heroines past shall not be in vain.
Regie:	Thanks for reminding me, Cheryl. Does this make sense to you, Sota? Engrave these ideals in your heart and hold it dear to you at all times.
Sota:	Sounds so easy to say, I tell you it is not as easy as you think. Well, I will do my best to realise your dreams.
Cheryl:	Your dreams?
Regie:	That's okay, Cheryl; our dreams will eventually become his dreams. I must be on my way. So long comrade, go in peace. You have my blessings. Do not let us down. I repeat, do not let us down. Sacrifice is the key, Sota. Labour now for a better tomorrow for us all. So long.

[He embraces Sota]

Cheryl, are you leaving with Sota immediately?

Cheryl:	We'll wait till the baby is born.
Regie:	That is fine. Call on me anytime you need my assistance. I am there for you.
Cheryl:	Thanks, Reji. I won't hesitate to call on you if need be.
Sota:	I will see you all before my departure. Bye and thanks for everything. I promise to live up to expectation. I will let no one down.

[Exit Regie]

Cheryl	Now that it is obvious nothing can stop you

	going home, what are your plans for the baby and I?
Sato:	Yes, back to the baby issue. I will leave for home next month and as soon as the baby is born, I will return to take both of you to Nigeria.
Cheryl:	Look here, Mr. Africa; I beg your pardon Nigeria. Our baby is due on 27th of May, so take a flight and be here on the 10th of May. A good politician must first be a good husband and father.
Sota:	What do you mean? Am I the midwife or the gynaecologist? Is it my job to cut the umbilical cord? What will I be doing hanging around the labour room?
Cheryl:	A lot, Dr. Sota. You have to be here when the baby arrives. Both of us have to be there for the baby. I think we have exhausted this topic. So see you on the 10th of May in preparation for your paternity task.
Sota:	Well, we will see about that. I'll see how that will work. I am already laden with a lot of tasks, which everyone expects me to perform excellently.
Cheryl:	That's up to you my prince of change. You've made your choice.

MOVEMENT 3

[Sota's home in Nigeria. His wife Aisosa looks stressed out. Wears a faded long skirt and blouse made from veritable wax wrapper. She serves him food, and then she sits to eat.]

Sota: Aisosa, what is this? Do you call this horrible thing food?

[Pushes the plate away]

The salt in the food is enough to season a 100kg of meat. Since I arrived, I have not eaten any decent food. It's either there is too much pepper, too much water and oil, no salt at all or too much salt. Aisosa, what happened to your culinary skills? You used to be such a good cook. Sorry, I have to go to a restaurant to find myself something to eat.

Aisosa: Well, please yourself. Since you arrived all you do around here is to condemn and complain about virtually every thing. It has become so difficult for anybody to please you. You are a different person from the Sota who left here some eight years ago. You are not satisfied with anything, no matter how hard we try. Please show some appreciation for our efforts. Your attitude scares the children away from you. Well, I think I am over stretched. I need to take my long deserved break now that you are here. Your complaining attitude is gradually wearing me out.

Sota: What do you mean by that? Of course, I have to complain. Things are not right here. Look at how lean the children are; see the tattered clothes they are in. Yes, look at the house too, bushy lawn, old shaky chairs, torn curtains, faded walls. I wonder how you live in here. This is nothing but a pig's sty.

Aisosa: What did you expect? Were you expecting to come into a palace, Dr. Sota Ojo?

Sota: I didn't expect to meet a palace or a castle, but I expected to be welcomed into a decent home, with healthy looking children, a pretty wife and a beautiful environment.

Aisosa: How was I to perform that magic, Mr. Fairy Godfather? You left here eight years ago for a PhD abroad, with the promise that you will send me money from your salary that was paid back home. Instead of four years, you ended up spending eight years and instead of the ₦40,000 monthly allowances you promised us, all you made available to us was ₦10,000 each month. And you have returned without a pin from Britain. So how am I to meet up with your standard, Sota Ojo?

Sota: Yes, but ₦10,000 is a lot of money.

Aisosa: *(Sarcastically)*

Yes, it is a lot of money to cater for four children, one house help, your sister, pay school fees for the children, maintain the house, care for your mother, pay doctor's and other bills.

Sota: You should have been doing something to make up.

Aisosa: Like what, Dr. Sota Ojo? Do what? When you asked me to resign my job as a consultant gynaecologist so I could give your children the best care they needed, did you not realise the implications?

Sota: You should have at least remodelled the house and made the children look better and brighter than they are now.

Aisosa: With ₦10,000?

Sota: But you never complained.

Aisosa: Complained to whom? Did I have your address? Didn't you ask your friends to keep it from me?

Sota: That is not true. I called occasionally.

Aisosa: Yes you did, from a phone booth and you spoke for 30 seconds as if someone put a gun to your head threatening to kill you if you didn't drop the phone. All I heard were excuses for your inability to return home.

Sota: *[Shouting]*

     Well, Aisosa you have no excuse for neglecting the house and the children the way you have done.

Aisosa: *[Standing up]*

     Mr. Sota, if anyone has neglected the home it is you. You walk in majestically, and no one opposes you, now you want to make my life miserable. I am sorry I won't take

21

that from you. You have no excuse for abandoning your family and home for eight years the way you did.

Sota: I am going to do just that again because I can't get satisfaction in here.

Aisosa: Do as you please. You did it before; you can as well do it again. It will be nothing new. We are already used to it. It is better than this daily complaints.

MOVEMENT 4

[Nosa's Office. Lavishly furnished.]

Sota: Nosa, I really appreciate your contributions to the success of my election as a senator.

Nosa: Well, you should show your appreciation to our wives. Aisosa and Ede mobilized the entire women of our senatorial zone and they responded in solidarity.

Sota: That is true. I was overwhelmed when I saw these women come out in their thousands to vote for me, even though it rained cats and dogs.

Nosa: Vote for you? No, they didn't vote for you, they voted for Aisosa. Our people have deep respect for Aisosa. They admire the way she comported herself in your absence. Some other women would have abandoned their responsibility and ran off with another man. She has been a good wife and mother, to you and your children, made a lot of sacrifices and the women wanted to reward, encourage and honour her by coming out to vote for you hoping that her lot will improve from now on.

Sota: But my people asked me to return home to become a senator.

Nosa: Did they? They didn't ask you to come home

to become a senator, they asked you to come home to contest for a senatorial position. How many of them came out to vote on that day? My friend, you must remain eternally grateful to Aisosa for this landslide victory.

Sota: Nosa, Aisosa may have performed marvellously in this election but in other aspects, she has failed wolfly. Look at my children; see my home, its all a sham.

Nosa: I am surprised to hear that from you. I expected you to organise a thanksgiving party to show your appreciation to Aisosa, for these eight years of holding forth for you. Sota, sincerely you should change your attitude and show a little bit of appreciation instead of this dissatisfaction and complaining. I am getting sick of it all.

Sota: Well, for your information I don't intend to take Aisosa to Abuja.

Nosa: *[Jumps up]*

What? Sota, are you out of your mind?

Sota: Nosa, I am very sane. I know what is good for me. I have my plans well laid out and Aisosa does not fit in anywhere. She does not befit my new status.

Nosa: New status? What do you mean, Sota? Aisosa does not deserve this treatment. You disappeared from the scene for eight years and when you returned you where presented with a house she built in your name, her parents died within a space of one year apart and you neither came nor sent her money for any of their funerals, she cared for your family, single-handedly raised funds for and organised your sisters wedding, nursed your mother here for four years while she was sick, and her reward for all is that she does not befit your new status, a status she facilitated? What is wrong with you, Sota? If you dare carry out your plan you will be disgraced.

Sota: What do you mean by that?

Nosa: You've heard me right, Senator Sota Ojo. I mean exactly what I have said.

Sota: To hell with any group of schemers. They can't do me any thing.

Nosa: Sota, I hope you realised that the women voted you into power.

Sota: So what?

Nosa: They can also pull the carpet off your feet.

Sota: They won't dare. What can women do in Nigerian politics?

Nosa: You are a *JJC*. The women have become very powerful over the years. They are a strong political force now, even though we fail to acknowledge it.

Sota: Really? They can't do anything. The men are still in charge.

Nosa: You may be right there, but the combined force of women can deal with you thoroughly

Sota: To hell with that bunch of good-for-nothing women, what can they do anyway?

Nosa:	You will see them in action when the time comes.
Sota:	Nosa, remember I have Cheryl to consider too. Our baby came in the heat of the election so I couldn't travel to London to be with her.
Nosa:	Sota, that is the greatest mistake of your life. You left your wife pregnant here in Nigeria to study abroad with the hope of returning after four years with a PhD; you decided to stay back and marry a white woman in Europe, abandoning your wife and children here. While you were away, this woman kept herself for you, but you were busy falling in love with another woman. You came back and she labours for you to win an election and in appreciation you ask her to leave your house because she does not befit your new position? Sota, remember, this woman was a consultant gynaecologist when you asked her to resign her job and stay home to care for your children. She would have become the Chief Medical Director of that hospital by now, considering the fast pace of her upward mobility. That is very cruel. Very, very cruel, Sota. You better reconsider your stand.
Sota:	Well there is nothing to reconsider. I cannot change my mind. It is made up. Aisosa no longer pleases me as a wife. If my white wife permits, may be I can consider keeping her in the house here in Benin.
Nosa:	Consider keeping her in a house she laboured to build in your name with the money she inherited from her parents? Remember, this

	woman is the only child of her parents; you are all she has for support. If nothing, consider all she did while you were away.
Sota:	She has not done anything extraordinary. Nosa, please I need your support now than ever.
Nosa:	Don't count on it. I will not be party to your wicked scheming. Look around your peers, how many people do you see marrying more than one wife? Polygamy is fast disappearing. It is no longer an option amongst our people here. Take a look for yourself and see if you can find any.
Sota:	I am not considering polygamy. I am doing away with Aisosa completely.
Nosa:	Well done superman. Does Cheryl know that you have a Nigerian wife here in Benin?
Sota:	How can? Who would have told her?
Nosa:	Then you are in for double trouble, Sota.
Sota:	It's not anything I can't handle with your support.
Nosa:	My what? You must be joking.
Sota:	Well, I will be away to London for two weeks to make arrangements for Cheryl to join me here as soon as we are sworn in and given a house in Abuja.
Nosa:	Sota, don't you have a conscience? Do you have no regard for God and His Judgement? Be careful, Sota. Give this plan another thought before you execute it. What if when you came home, Aisosa was involved in an-

other relationship or that she was married to someone else?

Sota: That would have been just right by me. Good riddance to an unbefitting wife.

Nosa: Be careful. Slow down, Sota. You are driving on the wrong lane. You better soft pedal and make a U-Turn.

Sota: Thanks for your advice; I am man enough to know what is good or bad for me.

Nosa: Good luck then my friend.

Sota: That is all I need from you.

[Lights out]

MOVEMENT 5

[Sota & Aisosa's home. It's night and Aisosa and Sota are in bed.]

Sota: Aisosa, why are you sweating like a Christmas goat? Look at your body you have developed folds everywhere. Your breasts are saggy, and you've put on weight. You sight irritates me, your body does not appeal to me at all.

Aisosa: *[Gets up, tries to subdue her obvious anger]*

Thanks for your compliments, Mr. Sota.

Sota: *[Shouting]*

Will you come back here?

Aisosa: Come back to where?

Sota: To bed, my bed of course.

Aisosa: Sorry, I am sleeping in the guest room. I'm sure you don't want this fat, old flabby bodied, saggy-breasted woman beside you.

Sota: Well, I have no choice, that's all I have for now.

Aisosa: Too bad, you may have to look elsewhere tonight because I am not coming back to that bed.

Sota: I'm sorry about that.

Aisosa: Apologies accepted. See you tomorrow morning.

Sota: You don't have to be mean.

Aisosa: What? Aisosa mean? I am sorry about that. Good night the father of my children.

Sota: Apologies not accepted. Please come back to bed. We will sort things out tomorrow morning.

Aisosa: Too late, Sota. Words are like water when poured on the ground, cannot be retrieved, sweet dreams.

Sota: How can my dreams be sweet without you by my side?

Aisosa: *[Laughs]*

            Me, Aisosa Ojo by your side, how romantic? You are already dreaming. I am not easily fooled. You can't lure me with your sweet words.

Sota: They did in the past.

Aisosa: That's true, when I was pretty, young and slim, but not anymore, Sota. Good night.

            [Shuts the door behind her and puts out the light]

MOVEMENT 6

[Sota is in the living room and Aisosa walks in tying a wrapper and blouse to match. Sota turns to look at her as she enters, obviously annoyed by her looks.]

Sota: What is this you are wearing? You look 60 years old for God's sake. Why can't you wear pants?

Aisosa: *[Shouting]*

          Sota Ojo, stop harassing my life, I've had enough. What do you take me for? I am a woman and not a girl, Sota.

Sota: I am not harassing you. You're my wife for heaven's sake; you have to dress to please me and not society. You are married to me, not society. Your attitude and reasoning must be aimed at pleasing me.

Aisosa: Thanks, Mr. Been-To. You have come too late. There is nothing wrong with my looks; rather you are the one with a problem. If you are so bent on changing my looks why didn't you make it a point of duty to buy me new clothes when you were returning from England? I won't become indebted simply because I want to please you my long lost husband. Since you returned, how much have you given the children and myself to buy clothes? Tell me how much?

Sota: How much does it cost to look good Aisosa? Look at you; from your head to your toes, you are ugly. You nauseate me. Your hair is always hidden in scarves. You tie wrappers all the time like a village woman.

Aisosa: Sota, in Africa, women dress as women not as girls. After eight years of your sojourn in Britain, how many fashionable clothes did you bring home for us!

Sota: Well, I didn't know your sizes.

Aisosa: Too bad, what a shame?

Sota: Sosa, I must be frank with you, you no longer excite me. You are too dull and drab. The spark that used to be in your life is no longer there.

Aisosa: No doubt, it's gone. What did you expect? Abandoned by a husband, no job, on a meagre allowance of ₦10,000 a month lost my dear parents who were so supportive, struggling to build a house for you and saddled with four children, did you expect to return home to meet a model? If you did, wouldn't you have been surprised?

Sota: *[Sighs]*

          Maybe, I should have taken you along.

Aisosa: Wishful thinking. Too late, Sota. Of course you don't mean that. You wanted to experience life and experiment with new things, you didn't want to be tied down or hindered by family responsibilities. After all some of your colleagues who value spousal relationship left with their wives and children.

Sota: That is no excuse for your becoming so drab. When I married you, you were so full of life, so much fun to be with. What has happened to you, Aisosa? Tell me, what happened to that Aisosa?

Aisosa: Sota, you murdered her. Of course, I was full of life; I was young, married to a visible person. My children had a father, your mother had a son and I had a husband, but for the past eight years ... I have been a father, mother, doctor, driver, tailor, nurse, extra lesson teacher, researcher, daughter in-law, sister-in-law, hair weaver and all others. All these took their toil on me as you can see.

Sota: Stop that, Aisosa, you drive me crazy; you are an absolute failure. You have failed as a wife; you have failed too as a mother. You cannot even meet my sexual needs. Sexually, you are dumb. Of what use are you as a wife?

Aisosa: I expected that from you, it has become your slogan. Sota, the sooner you learn that lovemaking is not jumping into bed with a woman at night, the better. My dear, it is a process and this process starts from the beginning of each new day. It is a holistic process. It involves your attitude, your mind, your mood, your physical being ... everything.

Sota: Enough of that, I am sick and tired of you, Aisosa. For your information I am filing for a divorce.

Aisosa: Well, I expected it earlier than now. I saw it

coming; I am not surprised at all. In any case, what have I done to warrant a divorce?

Sota: Everything in the book. I have just listed some of them.

Aisosa: Don't you think we should give ourselves sometime to renew our relationship for the sake of the children? Sota please be patient and don't be too hasty. Don't be selfish, Sota. The children need a father; they have never really had one.

Sota: No, I have had enough. You can keep the children; find them another father if you wish. Please stay out of my path.

Aisosa: So your mind is made up then?

Sota: Yes, it is. No going back. I want to move on with my life.

Aisosa: Oh! How remarkable. So I slowed you down? I have been a stumbling block on your path of success?

Sota: Yes you've been.

Aisosa: Well, since your mind is made up there is very little I can do. So be it then. When are you moving out?

Sota: Moving out? No, you are the one moving out with the children. I need my space. I am going to remodel this house to befit my new status.

Aisosa: Oh! Which house? My house? Sota. Where do you expect us to move to? To the street?

Sota: What do I care? It's between you and your

God.

Aisosa: Okay. I am sure God will take that up as a challenge. Should I expect any settlement?

Sota: Settlement for what? If you mean a small allowance for the children, I will consider that. My lawyer will be in touch with you.

Aisosa: *[Calm but sad]*

For the last time, Sota, do you think this is the right thing to do?

Sota: Of course it is. I am very confident in the decision I have taken. Please, keep your sympathizers out of my path because no amount of pleading will make me change my mind. This case is closed. Closed and it will remain so till eternity.

Aisosa: So be it then, what happens to my house? You remember that this house was built in your absence with the money I inherited from my parents.

Sota: *[Sarcastically]*

Dr. Aisosa, I am sorry I forgot about that. Please uproot your house out of my land before dawn. No matter what you do, please leave my plot of land intact.

Aisosa: Thanks, you can keep everything, the land and the house on it. God will avenge for me.

Sota: Amen. You need more than prayers. Goodbye. Please stay out of my life forever

Aisosa: Do you want us to leave today?

Sota: Yes, as soon as the children return from school. Well, you may leave tomorrow if it is too late. At least I concede that to you.

Aisosa: No thanks. I will start packing immediately. I am picking them from school on my way out.

Sota: With which car?

Aisosa: My car of course.

Sota: That's my car and not yours, remember?

Aisosa: But you gave my car to one of your political supporters.

Sota: That's true. You can get the car from him tomorrow; tell him I asked you to collect the car.

Aisosa: Is that so? You can keep the car then. Thanks and goodbye.

            [Exit]

Sota: Bye, Aisosa. Good luck to you.

            [Light fades out on Sota]

MOVEMENT 7

[Ede's home. She is reading newspaper in the living room as Aisosa enters.]

Ede: Hi sis. Give me a smile, will you?

Aisosa: *[Forces a smile].*

            Thanks, sis.

Ede: How was your day? I hope the car didn't give you any problems.

Aisosa: No, not at all. I am gradually getting used to driving in Abuja.

Ede: Thank God. I told you, you'd adjust.

Aisosa: I am happy I eventually followed your advice to relocate here.

Ede: How was the interview?

Aisosa: It was good, but hectic. There were a lot of younger doctors.

            [A screen shows the interview scene with smart looking young doctors queuing to be interviewed. Aisosa is there too]

Ede: What did they say?

Aisosa: The usual thing! "You've done very well, but you've been out of practice for too long. We don't want women above 30 years for this job".

Ede: Same as the other ones. Is it a crime to declare your actual age? Didn't you tell them you have passed all your professional exams and that you are over qualified for the job?

Aisosa: That makes no difference. The assumption is that I have lost touch with current practice. They have a point there. In medical practice, you can't break up half way to take a domestic leave for so long and expect to be accepted back so easily.

Ede: Well, that is why you are applying for a place as a company doctor and not the usual conventional hospital doctor.

Aisosa: It doesn't matter. Same rule applies. In all cases you are dealing with human beings even though it is just for minor ailments.

Ede: Never mind, Sosa, you are very young; you can still do a lot of things in your field.

Aisosa: What, at 41 years?

Ede: Of course you can. Never mind, as it is said "when the going gets tough, only the tough gets going, and tough times never last but tough people do", this tough time will be over soon. We will look back at this time in future and just laugh.

Aisosa: Yes, I strongly believe so. Thanks to your husband and yourself. You've been so wonderful. You have been such an encouragement. Where would I have gone?

Ede: You are welcome for as long as you want to stay. We don't need the guesthouse for now. So what is the next step?

Aisosa:	As we had discussed, I went to register in order to retake some of my professional examinations. I wonder how I will cope. Well, I've have bought the relevant books. There have been so many new developments in medicine since I left practice eight years ago. When I was in practice HIV/AIDS was not an issue but right now it has become a major issue with diverse implications. I met some doctors at the interview who have promised to put me through.
Ede:	Really? That is splendid. You are a very intelligent woman, Aisosa. Remember you passed your primaries and other exams in just one attempt each time. With a little more effort, you will upgrade yourself in no time.
Aisosa:	Ede, surprise, surprise! I have a job. Remember I was offering voluntary services at the Benin Branch of National Medical Research Centre? Well, the National Director was the Chairperson of the interview panel. He gave me a job there straight away.
Ede:	*[Jumps to embrace her]*
	Whoa! You should have told me that first, O thank God.
Aisosa:	The salary package comes to about ₦300,000 every month. That is not all; I will also help to manage the O&G clinic at his private hospital.
Ede:	Oh Aisosa, how did it happen?
Aisosa:	After the interview, he called me aside and said that the Director in Benin told him the

good work I did there without pay. He said he was told of the project I initiated. They had been looking for me since I left Benin. We went to the national headquarters where I was interviewed; my appointment was dated eight years back, that was when I started doing voluntary service for them. My arrears will be paid next week. I am to continue with the old project. Ede, I can now pay my children's school fees without any stress. That will relieve your husband and yourself of some burden.

Ede: Aisosa, I am so happy for you. Anything from Sota's lawyer yet?

Aisosa: Nothing, no money and no news about the divorce proceedings.

Ede: Guess what?

Aisosa: What?

Ede: My husband ran into Sota today. You know he has been avoiding him since we came to Abuja. This time he could not avoid Nosa. They discussed some issues.

Aisosa: What issues?

Ede: *[Laughing]*

The usual excuses. He said that you were boring in bed, you refused to satisfy his sexual desire, you are stubborn and that you are not submissive.

Aisosa: Nonsense, same old story, they all tell it. You see Ede, I always told him that lovemaking is more than sex, it is something that comes naturally from within, culminating in the fulfilment of both our desired pleasure. He demoralizes me everyday and expects me to be happy and excited at night, welcoming him to jump on me. No, I am not for that. He says I am old, faded, my body is ugly, my breasts are saggy, and that I have several folds on my trunk, then at night he wants me to obey his commands and jump on the bed to meet his sexual desires. No way, Ede. Am I a Zombie? No, I am human, with human feelings and desires yearning to be met too. I desire to be fulfilled as a woman. Any man will not robotize me.

Ede: That's true; men seem to forget that we are human too. My husband gets offended when I tell him I have backache or head ache at night. He calls it bedtime syndrome. Well, that's the only way I get him off my back.

[They both laugh]

Aisosa: We all do that. You see all a woman wants is to be loved and appreciated for who she is, period. Why would I sleep with a person who despises me and does not appreciate my person?

Ede: Take it easy, Aisosa. Aren't you lucky, you've been delivered from all that now?

Aisosa: I think I really am, at least no more disregard for my person and body.

Ede: Please, put all that behind you and move ahead, those who created the pain of the present do not control the pleasure of the future. Aisosa my sister, do not allow your past to hold your future hostage. Move on with your life.

Aisosa: Sometimes it is not so easy to move ahead. Can you still remember how Sota had always wanted me to resign from my job because he said it took too much of my time? He wanted me to be home always for the children. I finally gave in just before he travelled. He promised heaven on earth, but what happened after I resigned? The money he sent was just barely enough to pay the children's school fees and put miserable food on the table, nothing more. So how would I have cared for my body? If he wanted a beautiful woman he should have provided adequately for us.

Ede: I don't know why he is so selfish expecting you to be drowned in domesticity and motherhood and yet remain a model. If that is what he expected, he should have made adequate arrangements for that.

Aisosa: Ede, I suspect this is all a ploy. Some how, I feel that Sota is up to something. I regret resigning my job. I should have seen through him, and never have listened to him

Ede: Please let's forget about him *bo*! You know what Sosa? You are a very pretty woman, a medical doctor, a consultant gynaecologist, a researcher, and a mother of four beautiful children. What else can a woman ask for?

Aisosa: Thanks, Ede. I really appreciate your concern and encouragement; you've really helped to revitalise my self-esteem. I won't let you down.

Ede: That's my girl. No more tears now. Time

for weeping is over. You wept for three months in Benin and it didn't put food on your table. Now you are in Abuja, your land of promise. It's time to move ahead and show the world that you are not a failure. Put your past behind you but let it drive you to succeed.

Aisosa: You know what, Ede? I was not really weeping for Sota, after all he has never really been there for us. I wept for losing all I ever worked for, all I ever possessed, I wept for my house; it reminded me of my parents. I wept because I felt society would reject me. As you know, in our society, a woman bears all the blame when a family breaks up.

Ede: Says who? Was it not society that always admired your faithfulness to your husband and children, and stood by you during his election?

Aisosa: That is different, I was married then, now I'm separated and single.

Ede: It makes no difference. You're still same old Aisosa

Aisosa: Thanks. You make things look so simple.

Ede: Well Aisosa, there is something I must tell you, please don't get agitated. My husband asked me to keep it from you all this while, but I can't hide it any longer. It is eating me up.

Aisosa: What is it? Ede, you must know by now that I am through with Sota, I have de-programmed him from my system. As far as I am concerned, he is history now. Nothing is strong enough to harass me anymore; I 'm through with weeping. No more pity-party. When I left Benin, I left my mourning clothes and my bed of sorrow behind me. I left the memory of Sota Ojo behind me. I am here in Abuja for a fresh start and a new beginning. My eyes are set on the path of success.

Ede: Sota is married to a white woman. He married her while in Britain and she is leaving with him here in Abuja.

Aisosa: Oh my God, was that why he was looking for excuses to discard me? Ah, wonders will never cease. I wish him well. The woman is probably not aware that he is still legally married.

Ede: That is sure.

Aisosa: Sota! Sota!! He had better tread softly. He is really on the fast lane.

Ede: *Jo*, that's his business. He can drown in the ocean for all I care.

[Lights out]

MOVEMENT 8

[Sota's new house in Abuja. The furnishing reflects his new status as a Senator. He is getting ready to go out, Cheryl walks in holding a newspaper.]

Sota: Hi honey. How was your day out today?

            [Giving her a peck]

Cheryl: Fine. Everything went well. I am working on the first Lady's pet project on gender and the environment. It looks promising.

Sota: Sounds interesting. I am happy you are enjoying yourself. I was about to leave for a meeting

Cheryl: What? Starting a meeting this late? When will it end?

Sota: When ever it ends. That's politics for you.

Cheryl: Meetings don't have to be this late; after all today is a Saturday. How do the female members cope?

Sota: Just two of them, they have no choice. If they want to remain, they have to abide by the rules.

Cheryl: Rules made by men, that's not fair. You should adjust your time to suit them. Oh! By the way, why does the press address me as Mrs. Aisosa Ojo? I am not Aisosa my name is Cheryl. Look at it here in today's papers.

[Shows him the newspaper]

Sota: That's funny; there must be a mix up some-where.

Cheryl: A mix up with whom? This is the second time I've noticed it. The other day, your friend also called me Aisosa.

Sota: My friend? You mean Mr. Saye? What a coincidence? Don't work yourself up over such trivial matters like this. I will get my press secretary to put things in order. I'll see you as soon as we are done.

Cheryl: Okay then see you later. Don't stay too long.

[Sota exits]

There must be something wrong. I noticed Sota's countenance changed suddenly the moment I mentioned Aisosa. There is prob-ably more to it than he has explained. Isi is his cousin, she may probably be able to ex-plain what he called the mix-up. Isi! Isi!!

Isi: *[From afar]*

Yes madam.

Cheryl: Come right away.

[Enter Isi]

Isi: Madam, na me be this o.

Cheryl: Isi, do you know of any Aisosa?

Isi: No ma, I only know Esosa. But madam na who tell you say I know Aisosa? Na wa for people mouth o.

Cheryl:	You don't sound convincing.

Isi: Madam, na true true I dey talk o, I just dey here dey do my work for here *jeje jeje* o. Me I no be *olofofo* o, I no know anybody wey them call Aisosa. I no know who wan come put me for trouble o!

[Lifts one hand up as a mark of truth]

Cheryl: Isi, someone said you know Aisosa very well.

Isi: *[Pretending to cry]*

Oh God oh! Na who go do *amebo* for *oyinbo* madam, way e wan put me for trouble so o. Hey hey, na my job I dey do here *jeje* o.

Cheryl: Isi, who is Aisosa? If you don't tell me the truth, I will send you packing I don't care whether you are Oga's cousin or not.

Isi: Madam, me I don tell you say I no know any thing about any Aisosa o. Wetin you wan make I do now?

Cheryl: I am convinced you know more than you claim to know Isi.

Isi: Na wish kin thin be dis now? Make I kill myself before you believe me? Hey, hey, na who talk dis kin lie for my head?

Cheryl: It is Oga that said I should find out from you.

Isi: But Madam, why Oga no tell you himsef?

Cheryl: Tell me what? Oga left the house in a hurry. He left for an urgent meeting.

Isi: Dis kin thin no be the kin thing wey small *pickin* dey put mouth o. Me I no sabi di kin thin o. I no dey for trouble o.

Cheryl: As his cousin, you are the most qualified person to tell me about Aisosa.

Isi: Me I don tire for all dis lie lie. Wish kin *olofofo* them wan use me do so? Madam, true, true I no be Oga cousin. Na madam, Oga wife Aisosa na her bring me come here.

Cheryl: Oh my God! What? You mean Aisosa is Oga's wife? Oga had a wife before me?

Isi: Before nko? Wetin you think? Oga marry Dr. Aisosa well well. She born four children for Oga. Na doctor she be o, but Oga stop am from work. Dat woman

[crying]

na angel she be. I never see woman wey better like her. She suffer suffer follow oga but when oga come back from *oyinboland*, he come dey look for *cunny cunny* to drive am away because of you. Oga go say

[mimicking Sota]

Dis soup is salty; you are too fat, you are ugly. Your bodi dey smell, make you no tie your hair. Na wetin self? Nor do, no do, na so oga take drive am comot becos sey you dey come. Na so I see am o. Me I dey fear men o. See this woman don suffer suffer follow am now e say she no reach him class. Which kin class? God make you forgive me if my mouth don talk wetin e no suppose to say o, na di thing them ask me na him I talk o.

Cheryl: *[Looking very troubled]*

            Why did you not tell me all this while?

Isi: *Iyemwen* wish one be my own?, How I take
            know say Oga never tell you this before?
            No be you be him wife? Hey, wish one con-
            cern me? *Shoow*! I know wetin una dey dis-
            cuss for bedroom, I dey follow una sleep for
            there? Me, na my work I dey do *jeje* o. No
            be *amebo* them send me come do for here o,
            me I just dey here dey work make I collect
            my salary wey I go take complete school wey
            madam Aisosa put me o. Na God go fit me
            reward that woman.

Cheryl: That's all right. Isi, how can I get in touch
            with this Aisosa? I must see her don't you
            think so?

Isi: *[Stops to think]*

            I think say e go good make you see am.
            Madam Aisosa na very good woman. She
            no go fight you at all. The best thing be make
            you go see her friend Madam Ede.

Cheryl: Wait a minute, who is this Madam Ede?

Isi: Na Madam Aisosa correct friend.

Cheryl: That sounds okay do you know her house?

Isi: Me I nor know o.

Cheryl: Isi, where is Madam Ede's house?

Isi: Hey, hey, a beg madam nor put me for
            trouble o. I see her for market one day with
            Madam Aisosa.

Cheryl: Trust me, Isi, I will protect you.

Isi: Make you no tell Oga say na me tell you all this tory o, becos ebi like say no be Oga say make you ask me. I dey beg you please, I beg o.

Cheryl: Never mind; Oga will never know my source of information. I won't disclose my informant to him.

    [Laughs]

Isi: E good like that. I no know Madam Ede house, since dem come Abuja I only see her and madam Aisosa for market. E bi like say James, Oga driver know Madam Ede house becos e fit don carry Oga go there before.

Cheryl: Okay, that settles it. Who drove Oga out?

Isi: Na oga drive himself go out. Anytime Oga dress like young boy e nor dey gree make somebody drive am o. Hey, oga na show man o as you see am so. No be small thing madam Aisosa eye see o.

Cheryl: That's all right; call James for me.

Isi: Okay ma.

    [Lights out]

MOVEMENT 9

[There are 2 sets on stage. The frontal part of the gate to Sota's house & a moderately furnished office belonging to the women politicians. There are posters on the wall with slogans: POWER TO THE WOMEN, WOMEN ON A HIGHER MOVE, MOVING FROM MARGIN TO CENTRE, GIVE WOMEN A VOICE, LET A WOMAN SPEAK FOR YOU, VOTE FOR WOMEN & VOTE FOR A BETTER NIGERIA, WOMEN CAN LEAD TOO, WOMEN ARE HERE TOO, WOMEN ARE HERE TO STAY. There are at least 20 women in the gathering.]

Ma Speaker: Three weeks ago we sent Madam Power Power and Madam Executive to Abuja to see Senator Sota Ojo and Hon. Abel Nigie reminding them of the promises they made to us during their campaign. Their trip was a disaster. Well, madam, Power Power, is here, let her tell us about their experience.

Ma Power: My sisters, welcome to you all. Three weeks ago you mandated Madam Executive and I to go to Abuja to remind our two illustrious sons the promises they made to our people during their campaign. It's over two years now, we have neither heard from them nor seen them. Hon. Nigie received us very well, apologised for his inability to visit us for the past two years. You all know that he was sick for a long time. He has just returned from abroad where he went for treatment. He entertained us very well; in short we slept in his house. He will be meeting with our people in two weeks time. However, the story changed when we visited Dr. Sota. My sisters it is best you see for yourself what happened at Dr. Sota's residence.

[Scene moves to stage right in front of the gate leading to Dr. Sota's house. Madam Power Power and Madam Executive are outside the gate pleading with the Gateman, Aboki to open the gate.]

Aboki: Madam, I beg make una no vex, Oga no tell me say him been dey expect visitors.

Executive: We sent him a letter saying we were coming to see him, about four weeks ago. Go and tell him that the women from his constituency are here to pay him a solidarity visit.

Aboki: Madam, I know my Oga, e go ask me say whether him born *bomboy* way visitors dey come salute him.

Power: Tell him say Madam Power Power from Benin is here.

Aboki: If I go oga go ask me say whether any power pass him own for this house. Madam, I beg I dey respect una o. Please make una go look for phone call am. If e say make I open gate for una I go open am wide for una.

Power: Don't worry we have our phone here.

              [Brings out her cell phone]

              Give me his number.

Aboki: Madam, wish kin question be dis? Wish one concern *agbero* and overload? Wetin come join me and Oga *sotey* I come know him phone number. Madam, I beg make una hide my head o.

Executive: Aboki, you are stretching my patience. What do you want us to do now? We've been here for two hours and you have refused to grant us access to your mighty kingdom. Do you think we came all the way from Benin to play here?

Aboki: Wish kin trouble be dis? Na my fault say Oga no book una down for me? Wish one be my own inside? Me na gateman I be for here. I just dey follow my Oga instruction jeje o. A beg make una nor come put *san san* for my *gari* o. Una wan do una own job well well but una wan make I spoil my own. That one no good na. I get family for house o. If them drive me for here una go helep me feed them?

Power: Aboki, we are the ones who made your Oga a senator! Without our votes your oga would not have been here. If your oga were not here, you know you would not have been have been doing this job.

Aboki: Una do well for that one. But una see say me na the job wey them sy make I do na him I dey do I dey do for here. I no be politician. A beg make una no vex.

Power   Aboki, if you don't open this gate I am going to cause a stir here right away.

Aboki: Madam, I no get spoon to give you take stir any soup o. I no even get stove for you to cook any soup. If Oga catch you dey cook for here e go say you dey spoil him compound. You kuku ma know say na so so oyinbo na him e dey speak. Here na my duty post nor be woman kitchen.

Executive: Na you *sabi mai surutu*, talk talk.

Aboki: Madam na who teach you Hausa?

Executive: Shut up and open the gate.

Aboki: I don tell you say that one na *impossicant.*

Power: Okay then have it your way.

[Picks a big stone and starts banging it on the gate. Madam Executive blocks him from stopping Madam Power Power.]

Is anyone in this house? Open, we are visiting from Benin. Is any one in there? Open for your guests.

[She continues banging on the gate till Dr. Sota appears]

Sota: What is the matter? Who are you?

Power: *[Advances to embrace him, but Sota stops her]*

My Honorable Senator, it's me Madam Power Power. That is Madam Executive over there.

Sota: So what? I don't care who you are; you have no right disturbing the peace of my home. I don't even know you.

Power: Me, Madam Power Power? Sota, you don't know me? Well let me introduce myself, I am Madam Power Power the leader of the women group who voted you in as senator.

Sota: So? What is the big deal about that?

Power: Oh o, so becoming a senator in the Federal Republic of Nigeria is no big deal. All our efforts at bringing you to power is no big deal? You even refuse to recognise us, Dr. Sota, this amazing. I can't believe my eyes.

Sota: I careless. No matter who you are, you have no right to disturb my peace. Please take your leave.

[Walking away]

Executive: *[Who had been looking on in surprise, holds him back]*

You are not serious. Who are you to walk out on us? You are going no where until you attend to us.

Sota: Holding me hostage? Are you terrorists?

Power: Call us whatever you like, Dr. Sota, we would not let go of you until you attend to us. After all we notified you of our visit.

Sota: So what? Did I respond to your request? You cannot badge in on my privacy and expect me to attend to you. If you want me to attend to you come to my office on Monday.

Executive: And where do we sleep before Monday?

Sota: How is that my business, you should have thought of that before leaving Benin for Abuja.

Power: This is interesting; Dr. Sota you seem to have forgotten so soon how you used to bang on my gate at very odd hours just for us to strategise. Many times you woke me up at

12midnight, 2am, to quell the trouble brewing up in our camp. Neither my husband nor I complained. I didn't know you had such a short memory. You surprise me.

Sota: How dare you Madam Power Power insult me in my own home? Please leave my premises right away.

Executive: We are going nowhere. We are not leaving here. This is tax payers funded property

Sota: Then I have no choice than to have you arrested.

Power: Arrested? What crime have we committed?

Sota: Trespass.

Executive: Then forgive us this day our trespasses, lead us not into temptation. Forgive us our sins, Oga senator.

Sota: I have no time for cheap humour, women. Get off my premises or you face the consequences.

Power: We are seasoned politicians not makeover ones. So long as you have our mandate we won't leave your premises. The government gave you this house because we voted you into office.

Sota: Mandate? Whose mandate? What do I have to do with good-for- nothing women like you?

Executive: Mind your language Mr. Senator.

Power: Sota, have you lost your mind? Even if you have no respect for us because we are women, won't you respect the grey hair on our heads? Don't forget you represent our interest at the National Assembly.

Sota: Give me a break, would you? Must I lose my peace because I represent you at the National Assembly? Are you the only ones I represent?

Executive: No, but we worked hard for you. In any case we are here on behalf of the others.

Sota: Leave my home or you face the consequences.

Power: Consequences? O please, go ahead and do whatever you like we are equal to the task. We are going nowhere.

Sota: You asked for it. Aboki! Aboki!!

Aboki; Oga, na me bi dis.

Sota: Call me the police. I am going to teach these women a lesson they will never forget in their lives.

Aboki: H ee Oga, a beg o, dis small thing no reach to call police for. Una come from the same place o. Oga remember say you be politician o. Na politician bodi him people dey throway doti put o. Oga abeg dis women be like your mama dem o.

Sota: Will you shut your mouth! Do as I say and don't you dare question my authority.

Aboki; Okay, Oga, na you get power, no vex o.

[As he leaves, he secretly makes signs to the women to leave]

Power: Sota Ojo, do whatever you like we are not leaving here.

Sota: Okay then have your way. You asked for it.

[They all freeze and light fades out on them. Light comes up gradually on the the women politician giving Madam Power Power and Madam Executive time to join the others on the set.]

Power: That was how the policemen came and arrested us charging us with disturbance of peace and trespass of private property. We sent for some women politicians but they were not allowed to bail us. So my children sent us a lawyer who finally bailed us after much *wahala.* My women that was how we were detained in the cell for three days simply because we went to persuade Senator Sota Ojo to fulfil his promises to our people.

Women: *[In reaction to Madam Power Power's speech, some sigh, some weep, others make various exclamations]*

Show Dem: Na wa for dis Dr. Sota o. Na so somebody fit change overnight? No bi dis Sota wey e go laugh with us, chop for the same plate with us na him just change like dis? God I beg o.

Speaker: So my women what do we do? Do we send Sota congratulatory card for what he has done?

All: God forbid bad thing.

Speaker: Then speak up. What then do we do? Do we allow Sota Ojo to continue riding on his high horse? My sisters, do you realise that Dr. Sota drove Aisosa to the street two years ago and brought in a white woman?

Women: *[Show surprise]*

Speaker: Any man who cannot stay with Aisosa must have a problem.

Executive: I know Aisosa is such a sweet girl. See how many years she waited patiently for him.

Power: And what was her reward?

Speaker: Robbed her of all her possession, and threw her out on the street.

Show Dem: Make una lef am, God no dey sleep.

Executive: That man must be callous.

Power: He is mean. He has no conscience.

Executive: If Aisosa had come to report this case to us when it happened we would have doubted her testimony. We would have said she is not patient enough. Our experiences of last three weeks have left us without any doubt as to who Senator Sota is.

Show Dem: My people make una forget Sota. If person get broda, you no dey ever see de broda, you no dey hear from am, no be say she no get broder be dat?

Women: That na true talk.

Show Dem: Person wey e no get pocket betta pass de one wey e get and him own get hole, nor bi so?

Women: Na so.

Power: *[Standing]*

What I will say is for us to give Sota a long rope and give him an opportunity to tender us his apologies.

Executive: Senator Sota Ojo apologise to 'good-for-nothing-women'? You must be dreaming.

Speaker: The essence is not that we want his apologies badly but for us to follow due process. Who know, he may have repented but is ashamed to come out to apologise. So let us help him by giving him this opportunity. We will write to him, Secretary!

[She steps forward from the crowd]

Write to Sota saying that we demand a written apology from him.

Show Dem: As for me I for sey make we show am say we be women with power, better power and authority, sey we no be bottom power women o, but women with correct power.

Power: Let's give him the opportunity to apologise first.

Executive: What if he doesn't?

Speaker: We shall cross the bridge when we get there. Do we all agree?

All: Yes.

[Lights out]

MOVEMENT 10

[Ede's living room. Ede is seen doing some calculation on her calculator. There is a knock on the door.]

Ede: Come in!

            [Enter Cheryl and Isi, they exchange pleasantries]

Ede: Hello, what can I do for you?

Cheryl: You probably may already know that I am Cheryl Ojo, the wife of Senator Sota Ojo.

Ede: So what? I hope you are aware that you are in the wrong home. This is the residence of Engr. Nosa Iyayi.

Cheryl: I understand why you are putting up this attitude. It may interest you to know that I am here as a friend, Isi told me about Aisosa and advises that I should see you.

Ede   I see *[Ede's Phone rings]* Hello! Oh! Where have you been? Okay you are on your way here? Oh! No no..yes. Eh okay! No, I'm home. Okay! Okay! Oh, very close to the house… Well Okay, Okay … yes! Yes!… I have some guests… Yes, the appointment is still on …okay, I'll expect you.

Isi: Na wah oh!

Ede: You are welcome. Well there is nothing more

to know. It is obvious Isi has told all there is to know. I hope you are aware that Dr. Sota is still legally married to Aisosa. They got married in Benin before he left for England. Fortunately when he drove her out of the house we were moving to Abuja, so she moved along with us.

Cheryl: You mean he drove her out on the street? Why would he do a thing?

Ede: Just for Lady Cheryl's sake. So he could bring you in.

Cheryl: For my sake? What the hell does he mean? Oh my God! What can I say?

Ede: Are you telling me that you know nothing about this?

Cheryl: Absolutely nothing. I only heard about Aisosa today. I never even knew he had any child before.

Ede: He has four children by Aisosa, three boys and one girl. The oldest is twenty and the youngest is ten years.

Cheryl: You mean Sota has four grown up children? Oh my God! Oh my God!

Ede: Exactly, four grown up children.

Cheryl: *[Crying]*

Oh my God! What a mess? Where is Aisosa? You think she will be willing to see me?

Ede: Well I can't say. All I know is that she has gotten over the whole affair. She is on her feet again and has put the whole episode behind her.

[Knock on the door]

Come in!

[Enter Aisosa, looking cheerful and dressed smartly]

Aisosa: Hi everyone

[Stops as she notices Cheryl]

You must be the Lady Cheryl.

[Cheryl moves to her, embraces her and weeps on her shoulder]

Cheryl: Yes I am. Please forgive me Aisosa. I never knew Sota had a wife before I married him, I am really sorry.

[Weeping]

Aisosa: It is really no fault of yours. It's okay. That's fine.

[Trying to comfort her]

Cheryl: I am sorry to have caused you so much pain. I wish I had a hint of it. I always knew there was something undisclosed eating up Sota, but I could never put my finger to it. He always put up his tough look as cover up.

Aisosa: Well it has happened. There is nothing you can do about it.

Cheryl: No, certainly there is something I can do about it. Of course I can't continue to live in this fool's paradise; I must leave immediately and seek for a quick divorce or an annulment.

Aisosa: Cheryl, please take it easy don't be too hasty. You need time to think things over before you act.

Cheryl: Think things over? There is nothing to think over here. In the first place our marriage is noil and void. In any case if I don't leave this country in the next two days I may end up shooting Sota. So, the earlier I leave the better for all of us.

Ede: It is better you act as you think best. We are here for you and will support you all the way. You can count on us.

Cheryl: Please Aisosa, can you do me a favour?

Aisosa: And what is this favour?

Cheryl: I have a two and a half year old daughter, Rieme; I would appreciate it if you can take care of her for me. I want to move ahead with my life with out any memory of Sota and his deceit. He has deposited ten million pounds in my London account, which he claims he got from an oil contract and was paid just two weeks ago. I am handing every penny over to you. You need to come to London latest next week so we can finalise the transaction. I don't want a penny from his money. I can move on without him.

Aisosa: Thanks, Cheryl, that's very kind of you. But, I really don't need that money. I just got a job at the medical Research Institute. I have a handsome grant; our overseas donor and the government pay me. That is more than enough to take care of the children and me, including your daughter.

Cheryl:	If you don't take the money I will give it to charity in my country.
Isi:	A beg madam, make you go take the money now.
Ede:	Well in that case, she will take the money and use it for his children
Aisosa:	No, I don't want anything from Sota Ojo. I have survived this far without him. I do not need any money from him.
Ede:	Shut up! You will take the money. Cheryl, go ahead and process the transfer. We will sort things out here. Aisosa will be with you in London next week.
Aisosa:	Ede, don't be too hasty. Do you realize that that is our government money? We will become like him if we accept this obviously ill acquired money.
Ede:	So what do you suggest, that she gives the money away to charity in her country just like that when we have millions dying here?
Aisosa:	There you go. Cheryl, do us a good favour; return the money to our government account.
Cheryl:	That's fine by me. I will do just that. I have to rush to the embassy. Sota may cease my passport when he discovers I am leaving. So I need to get new travelling documents to exit.
	[They all embrace]
Ede:	Bye girl. Take care of your self.

Cheryl: Bye sisters. I will be fine.

Aisosa: Bye now, Isi thank you.

            [Isi and Cheryl exit]

Ede: Aisosa my sister, wonders will never end. You
            mean that man had so much money and he
            never provided for his children? Good gra-
            cious. Aisosa, this calls for a celebration.
            Let's go out.

Aisosa: What is there to celebrate? That Sota suc-
            ceeded in fooling both of us for six years?

Ede: You are better off for it, Ede.

Aisosa: I feel so sorry for Cheryl. I hope she doesn't
            do anything funny.

Ede: I don't think she would. I beg let's go to
            mama Tope's restaurant for pounded yam,
            egusi soup and cold kunu drink.

            [Lights out]

MOVEMENT 11

[Sota's house, sitting relaxed with his legs stretched and watching television, enter Cheryl with Isi sneaking behind her.]

Sota: Why were you out for so long? You left Rieme alone with that girl that doesn't know her left from her right.

Cheryl: When did you become such a loving father? What do you care about children? Go care for your abandoned wife and four children, Mr. Senator.

Sota: *[Shocked, jumps up]*

            What?

Cheryl: You heard me right, bigamist. You thought I would never know. You think I am a fool? It is a small world you know. Honourable Dr. Senator Sota Ojo. How appropriate? For six years we have been married and you cleverly kept this a secret. Today your secret is out. Blown out by the wind of destiny. Your can of worms has been thrown open to the view of all, Sota.

Sota: Well, I can explain.

Cheryl: Explain what? Too late Sota, too late. It is six years belated. There is nothing to explain.

            [Starts to make for the door]

Sota: *[Holds her back]*

But I did all these for your sake.

Cheryl: For me? You deceived me for my sake? That's not true. I met the real Aisosa today. Such an elegant lady, have you seen her recently? She is so glamorous, looking like a movie star!

Sota: So you are in touch with Aisosa.

Cheryl: Oh of course, Sota. A wonderful woman, pretty young lady, Sota you are wicked and heartless? You must be the devil himself to have abandoned such a sweet, pretty lady and her four children. [counting her fingers] Four children, Sota.

Sota: That's enough, madam. I do not need you to lecture me on morals. So both of you have finally met en hn? The cat is out of the bag eh? I am now an enemy to you both?

Cheryl: Enemy? No way. You are the father of our five children you deceived us though. You fooled us all for six years, Sota.

Sota: I am an African. My father married six wives. Every father prays for his child to perform better than himself. Polygamy is no crime in Africa, Cheryl.

Cheryl: Says who? Stop deceiving yourself.

Sota: Says my African culture.

Cheryl: Stop hiding under the cloak of culture, Sota. Your father never deceived his six wives; he married them according to the prevailing traditions of his time. No culture tolerates deceit. For your information you've violated the CEDAW convention.

Sota:	To hell with CEDAW. My country knows nothing about CEDAW.
Cheryl:	Your country is a signatory to it.
Sota:	That will not work with me.
Cheryl:	Then you must be heading for jail. In Britain where were married, polygamy is an offence. My Father married one woman.
Sota:	That's your business. I am not British.
Cheryl:	Shut up criminal. You have no conscience Sota. You have the guts to celebrate your evil and glory in it? I wish you well Mr. Senator. The next time you step into Britain you will spend the rest of your life in jail.
Sota:	What do you mean, Cheryl?
Cheryl:	Exactly what I have said. Well Sota, I am done with you. I cannot take this. I will be out of here tomorrow.
	[Leaves, Sota reaches for her hand and pulls her back]
Sota:	Not so fast, Lady. Where do you think you are going? You will leave this country only when I say so. I have your passport remember?
Cheryl:	You can keep it. I don't need it.
Sota:	O my God, this is no longer a joke.
Cheryl:	You bet.
Sota:	Cheryl, please don't go away, stay here with me. I have given up so much for your sake.
Cheryl:	Liar! For your ego you mean? You wanted

class, so you used me as a sacrificial lamb to climb the social ladder. Heartless social climber.

Sota: Whatever, please stay back. We can work things out.

Cheryl: Why didn't you work things out with Aisosa? What crime did she and your children commit?

Sota: Well, Aisosa is past, let's talk about us now.

Cheryl: Yes, talk about us because I have your money. Too late Sota, too late. You've lost the money. My bank has already transferred it to the rightful owner. I cannot even cash a penny out of it even if you keep me back here. If you dare prevent me from travelling, I will sell your story to the press. What a good headline it will make, "The Chief Whip of the House of Senate involved in cross-cultural bigamy scandal and has 10 million pounds lodged in a London account".

Sota: Has it come to that?

Cheryl: Yes, you go-getter. You are not as smart as you think after all. Your castle has crumbled.

Sota: My God! My God! I am dead.

Cheryl: Yes, dead and buried with your legs sticking out of your grave. Sorry, I have to go to bed. Tomorrow is a busy day for me. You will be hearing from my lawyer Mr. Bigamy.

Sota: Too bad. Women, how terrible?

[Sota sinks into the sofa with his head buried in his hands]

MOVEMENT 12

[Ede and Nosa's House. Nosa is on the phone as Aisosa rushes in.]

Aisosa: Nosa! Ede! Ede!! Nosa!! Thank God for me, I have made it! I have finally made it. It is a major break through. I got a letter from the United States today saying that I have received an award for leading an exemplary life in the face of adversity. Cheryl led a coalition of groups and organisations to put me up for the award. I am getting $300,000. Oh Nosa, God is faithful. By the way where is Ede? Ede! Ede!!

Nosa: Whoa! Congratulations! Ede went out and will be back shortly. Aisosa I am very happy for you.

[Ede rushes in joyfully and embraces Aisosa]

Ede: My sister, I heard it on the radio. The world is rejoicing with you Aisosa. Do you know that the president of the country is giving you a reception tomorrow at 7 p.m.? Oh Aisosa, I am so happy for you.

[They embrace each other again]

O Aisosa, all these years of hard work and self-denial have paid off after all.

Ede: You will be receiving the award in New York next week.

Aisosa: Whoa! Oh, what can I say? Really? Am I dreaming?

Ede: No, you are not. You are wide-awake.

[They embrace weeping]

Aisosa: Nosa and Ede, I am dedicating this award to you, thanks for your support. I will never forget you both. Thanks to Sota for throwing me out on the street when he did, and thanks to you for persuading me to move with you to Abuja. That decision has brought a change in my life. You have been so helpful. I will appreciate it if both of you can accompany me to receive this award.

Ede: O really? What an honour? We will be glad to. You deserve the award Aisosa. You have been so faithful.

Nosa: That's right, you deserve it, Aisosa dear. Above all you deserve the award for being the best mother and the best wife.

[They all laugh]

Aisosa: Yes, the best wife that Sota never had.

[They all laugh]

Ede: Whatever. He has lost out. You see what he meant for evil has open international doors for you. Time to celebrate *jo*. I have asked my driver to bring your children from school. How is baby Rieme?

Aisosa: Fully adjusted. She even calls me mama now. Hardly asks for her mum. She started school last week.

Ede: Ah yes, have you called Cheryl?

Aisosa: I called immediately I got the news. It was then she confessed her role in suggesting that I be nominated for the award. She is travelling to France tomorrow for a well-deserved vacation, and she may probably relocate there.

Ede: I am sure she wants to put the past behind her.

Aisosa: Yes, she wants to forget her experiences down here. She will call me in New York.

Nosa: Too bad, I wish her well. Let's go out and celebrate.

Ede: We cannot go out. The press will disturb us. Do you know that we have a celebrity with us?

Nosa: Oh my God, I forgot. Well, we can still manage to sneak somewhere very secluded.

Aisosa: Please don't be funny, Ede. Let's go anywhere you choose, they don't know me.

[They all laugh and lights fade out]

73

MOVEMENT 13

[Aisosa's House. Very well furnished. The television is on. Ota, Aisosa's son is watching the television.]

Ota: Mummy! Mummy!! Come over come fast.

                [Aisosa rushes to the living room]

Aisosa: What is on? What? What?

Ota: Daddy has lost his seat at the senate; he has been recalled.

Aisosa: Oh my God. Why? Why?

Ota: They said a group of women from his senatorial zone mobilized people and signed a petition asking that he be recalled from the National Assembly.

Aisosa: O, no, why? Why? Oh my God.

Ota: But mum, why are you so concerned after all he's done to you?

Aisosa: He is your Father, Ota. Show some sympathy.

Ota: Sympathy? Daddy deserves what he got. He needs to learn that he doesn't own the whole wide world, and that it does not revolve round him alone. Did you hear that he got some women from his constituency arrested for going to visit him; he got them arrested for trespassing his property and encroaching on his privacy. They were detained for three days. There days mum. It is a pity that this is happening at this time anyway.

Aisosa: What? Three days?

Ota: Are you surprised? Don't you know your husband? Did he not drive you out on the street? Serves him right.

Aisosa: How has Sota changed since he came into power!

Ota: Which power? Was he in power when he abandoned you here in Nigeria and married another wife in England?

Aisosa: Yes that was power too.

Ota: I wonder where a fine woman like you came across a man like Sota Ojo. Sometimes I wish he were not my father.

Aisosa Unfortunately, he is still your father. That is a fact you will never be able to change. Please try to give him a call before you leave.

Ota: Mum, we are leaving tomorrow I don't have much time. I am sure Ifueko will make out time to call him. There is no need to pamper him, let him suffer the consequences of his many atrocities.

Aisosa: That is not fair.

Ota: Sometime you have to let people reap the fruits of what they have sown, that way they come out better.

Aisosa: This will break Ifueko's heart.

Ota: She can stay back and lament with a father

	who does not care a thing about her, for all I care.
Aisosa:	Your dad's life is gradually crumbling.
Ota:	Gradually? It has crumbled. Life is closing in on him, he had better retreat fast and make amends or he will be crushed against the walls of evil he built around himself.
Aisosa:	How sad. Ota, he needs your support in times like this.
Ota:	Did I ever get any from him? He hardly knows me we are like two strangers. His mother rather stays here with us than go to him. Can't you see how close both of you are in spite the fact that you are her daughter-in-law.
Aisosa:	Try not to be bitter, Ota. You will get over all these.
Ota:	What do you mean can he rewrite the past?
Aisosa:	Where is Ifueko?
Ota:	She went for last minute shopping and visiting.
Aisosa:	Trust Ifueko, and Ibude?
Ota:	They went out together.
Aisosa:	All right then, I am going to the clinic. I have a caesarean section waiting for me. See you later
Ota:	Bye mum.

MOVEMENT 14

[Aisosa is in her study. The study is attached to the living room. She is working on the computer. Ede enters with two older women.]

Ede: Hi sis. How are you? Have you heard from the children?

Aisosa: Yes, they called a few minutes ago. They are adjusting well. I miss them though; Ifueko was such a good manager of my affairs. She made life easy for me.

Ede: Never mind. Iro will help take charge of the house, since Isi is back to school now.

Aisosa: Yes, she will. My mother –in-Law is coming over next week too. I got a live-in house-keeper for the children over there so they can have little or no distraction. She is a wonderful woman. [She suddenly notices the women and embraces them]   Ah!   I am sorry, good evening ma. I got carried away, and forgot my manners. Please, forgive me. Madam Power Power, how are the grandchildren? Madam Show Dem, how is your family? It's so nice of you to pay me a visit.

            [They all exchange pleasantries]

Aisosa: What can I offer you?

Power: Aisosa, sit down, we don't have much time. We spent the whole day trying to locate your

	house. Ede's house was all we could locate she is kind enough to bring us here. We must return to Benin this evening.
Aisosa:	No, it's too late. Please, spend the night here; there is enough room for everyone.
Power:	Thanks for your hospitality, but we can't accept such luxury. Aisosa, my dear we are here for business. Our group has asked that we request you to vie for the vacant senatorial seat in our zone.
Aisosa:	*Iye mwen!* You mean Dr. Sota Ojo's seat? What?
Power:	Yes, you heard me right. That's the seat Dr. Sota was recalled from.
Aisosa:	And you want me Aisosa Ojo to take up his seat? Ah! *Iye,* you know I wouldn't do that.
Show Dem:	Why?
Aisosa:	Why? In the first place I am engaged for now, my hands are full. I love my job; I enjoy it. Secondly, what will society say if I do such a thing?
Ede:	Let society be stuffed. Society will always have something to say.
Power:	Would you rather a complete stranger take up the post?
Aisosa:	I don't care who takes the position but please leave me out of it.
Show Dem:	No we won't. You see we have no other person who is competent enough to represent us at the Senate. You are the most appropri-

ate person. See all your recent achievements, with such feats, when you talk on the floor of the Senate men are bound to stop and listen. So, this has nothing to do with Sota.

Aisosa: Well, society will see it differently. Oh dear! *Iye*, please, leave me out of this. I am just not prepared for it.

Power: Leave that to us. We will prepare you. All we need is your consent.

Aisosa: *Iye*, this is a really difficult situation. I would prefer to keep off.

Power: You can't keep off my dear; we all have a duty to serve our people.

Aisosa: *Iye*, please leave me out; I don't to be messed up in this. Sota will think I spearheaded his recall. *Iye*, for heaven's sake deliver me from the impending tongue-lashing that is bound to follow.

Power: You better brace up because we have no other alternative.

Aisosa: O my God, *Iye*, why me? There are better people, women and men.

Show Dem: We know, dis time na woman we want. So make you go prepare o.

Aisosa: *Iye*, I must be frank with you, this is tough. The whole world will turn against me. I will have a hard time exonerating myself from his removal plot. No, *Iye*, please find some-one else.

Show Dem: Aisosa, my *pickin*, we too we pity you, we don think over am too. But you see, if we no bring someone like you wey e be winning card, another local government fit carry am from us. So you see am my *pikin*?

Power: Look here, Aisosa my dear, let people say whatever they like, we have a constitutional right to recall anyone we feel is not representing our interest at the National Assembly. Politicians just have to learn that their job is to represent their people's interest, and not to go there and represent their personal interest. Anyone who misbehaves will be dealt with decisively, even you my Aisosa.

Show Dem: Dis na de time for serious business. You know say no bi only us choose you o, our party send people to go ask all around who dem want, you know say all our people for *oyinboland* say na you, the ones for here say na you, both women and men. So you see say we just come here as our people messengers.

Power: That is true. We are actually here on behalf of our party, not as grassroots' women group. You know what? We will give you one week to think it over. We must send a name to the NECOM (National Electoral Commission) in ten days time.

Ede: *Iye,* I think that is better. We will get back to you before the end of one week.

Power: Aisosa, is that okay by you?

Aisosa: *Iye,* you don't give up. Do you?

Power: Why should I?

[Moves over to Aisosa]

We are expecting your response Aisosa.

Aisosa: That's okay.

Show Dem: We must be on our way then.

Aisosa: *[Runs into an inner room]*

              Just a minute.

              [Aisosa returns with two new lace wrappers and nylon bags which she hands to the two women]

Aisosa: Thanks *Iye*, I appreciate your confidence in me. I will give your request a deep thought, tough though it may be. Have a safe trip home.

Show Dem: Thanks my *pikin*, you do well. Make you nor worry, we go help you. Make we hear you soon o.

              [Aisosa shakes her head in response]

Power: *[Moves over to Aisosa and parts her shoulder]*

              Don't forget we are expecting to hear from you soon.

Aisosa: *Wa ruese*. I won't forget. Thanks and have a safe trip.

Show Dem: Bye Aisosa, bye Ede.

              [Exit Madam Power Power and Madam Show Dem, as they leave Aisosa slumps into the chair. Ede moves closer to her]

Ede: Sosa dear, I know how you feel, but please let's not fail our people.

Aisosa: How can you talk like that? Ede, you know all I went through to rebuild my career, how

	difficult it was to get back into medical practice? You want me to throw that away just because these women have come knocking?
Ede:	Yes, one good turn deserves another. When you needed their support to vote for Sota, they all came out to support and vote for him. Now they want you to come in his place and you say no?
Aisosa:	Why do I have to smear my name and allow myself to be ridiculed for nothing? What do I need Politics for? I am fulfilled professionally and financially. I am well known in my field nationally and internationally.
Ede:	Yes. That is why they need you.
Aisosa:	Ede, why do you want to disrupt my life at this point? Do you know what you are asking me to do? To put aside my career, and step into politics. That is a huge sacrifice.
Ede:	Yes, our people deserve that sacrifice. They need credible people like you. Please don't fail them. You have nothing to worry about. Your three big children are studying abroad. The two small ones here are well cared for by Isi and Iro. Your mother – in –law will be arriving soon. You can still maintain light schedules at your work place and the clinic, so you can keep in touch with your medical practice.
Aisosa:	It's easy to say that now.

[Pauses]

This is incredible. I can't believe this is happening to me. Not again.

Ede:	Never mind. It will be well. Take care, Sosa; I am going home.
Aisosa:	Thanks, Ede. I will call you later.
Ede:	Bye, be a good girl and give it a thought.

[Exit]

MOVEMENT 15

[Sota's living room at his home in Benin. The environment is looking unkempt, Sota looks haggard and frustrated. He has on a rumpled shirt and pair of trousers.]

Sota: *[Seated on a settee, gazing into space, occasionally he sighs and shakes his head]*

Five million naira, only five million naira and no one is willing to assist me. Its sad, no one. I've just till tomorrow noon to pay or this house will be gone. Gone, that's it, gone to the highest bidder.

[Knock on the door]

Yes, come in. I say come in. The door is open, come in or leaves me alone.

[Enter Nosa and Regie]

Oh so good to see you both.

[They embrace him]

How come both of you are together?

Regie: Sota, Sota, how are things with you?

Sota: Bad, really bad. I am in a terrible state. Things have gone very bad; my friends in high places wouldn't even pick my calls. I am neck deep in debt. Well, I am sorry to bore you with my story. Regie, what are doing in Nigeria?

Regie:	I told you we would return to serve the nation and to assist you. I am here for good; my family will join me as soon as I settle down. I am here to stay. Home is where we all belong Sota; the country needs us. This is the only home we have; we have no other one. Things may not be as rosy as we expect; but if we all do our part, things will improve. Our space is within this country.
Sota:	That is very true though. Sometimes I wonder if this country deserves such a huge sacrifice from us. Look at me for instance, I have lost all just because I abandoned base in England to come home to serve my country.
Nosa:	Sota, your case is different.
Regie:	Sota, what happened? What went wrong?
Sota:	My brother, I was victimized, set up by some women here. They connived with Aisosa and pulled the carpet from under my feet.
Nosa:	For once Sota be sincere with yourself and tell the truth, we are no strangers. How can you blame Aisosa for your mistakes? You know what you did, why put the blame on someone else? Accept your faults and rise above it. Did I not warn you in this same city about those decisions you took? For once show some maturity and be honest with your self.
Regie:	I remember you told me while you were still in London that Aisosa had abandoned you to leave with another man. What was the use of lying? You were never really with us Sota. You fooled all of us. We supported you,

I spearheaded your fund raising campaign in London, so you could come back here and represent our people very well and help transform our nation. But Sota, I was wrong, my expectation of you was lofty. I should have known.

Sota: Please, hear me out, Regie. Don't come here to condemn me, you are all I have now. Look around you, there is no one left, not even the cook, steward or *maiguard*. They have all abandoned me. I am all by myself. I have no food, no water, and no electricity. The bank will impound this house tomorrow by noon if I do not sell it to pay up the loan I took before I left for Britain. Small amount then, I used the land papers to secure the loan. So here I am in desperate, without anyone to help. I had forgotten about the loan, but immediately I was recalled and I returned to Benin, they pounced on me. I am very sure Aisosa is behind all these. She built the house. She probably would have reminded the bank of the loan so she can buy back the house. It's a wicked world.

Nosa: Sota, you know Aisosa would never do such a mean thing. She has several houses, moreover, she has long forgotten about you and the house. She doesn't even remember that she was once married to someone like you. The children are the only reminder, o, and maybe your name.

Sota: I will reclaim the name from her very soon. Yes, she has to stop using my name.

Regie: So what? What will that do to her? What is in your name? She is not a bastard; she can use her father's name. Was that why you started using a compound name, so you could cut her off? Sota, grow up man. You are too petty.

Sota: Yes, I had to do that to teach her a lesson. The children refused to obey me by fixing the new addition to their name. That is Aisosa for you, she has brainwashed the children. She is so full of herself, very proud and arrogant. All she does is advertise herself. She thinks that appearing on television and cover page of the newspaper is all there is to life. Everywhere you go in Abuja all people talk about is Aisosa Ojo. She had better be careful.

Regie; You've got some problems man, you are feeling threatened by someone who has long forgotten about you. if you don't watch it you will end up in a mental home. You have an attitude. I can't stand this. Sota what has taken hold of you? Please go clean up your attitude.

Sota: Aisosa has ruined my life.

Nosa: How?

Sota: You should be the one to tell me. You connived with her. I heard all both of you did. I thought we were friends. You backstabbed me. I wish you all well.

Nosa: Sota what nonsense are you talking about?

Sota: *[Talking to Regie]*

You see, Nosa has always been envious of me, but I didn't expect he would take my wife. Nosa, why did you do it?

Nosa: Do what, Sota? Are you out of your mind? Regie, I think I have overstayed my welcome in this house. I beg to take my leave. I can't stand this anymore.

[Rises to go but Regie motions him to sit down]

Regie: Sota, I can't pay your bank loan, but at least I can give you some money to survive on. Get someone to clean up this place and bring in your mother to cook for you.

Sota: *[Laughs]*

My mother? My mother and Aisosa are best of friends, since Aisosa left, the only time I saw my mother was when I was recalled, and all she said was that I deserved what I got. She spends most of her time with Aisosa.

Regie: That is so sad. Your situation is pathetic.

Sota: I don't need sympathy. All I need now is support in its entirety.

Regie: I am sorry; you don't behave like someone in need of assistance.

Sota: Well, I am not prepared to crawl to anyone simply because I need assistance.

Nosa: Sota, you need help. Go for it fast.

Sota: I don't blame you, Nosa; I blame Aisosa, Madam Power Power and their cohort. The wall has fallen down flat so the goat can climb on it anyhow.

Nosa: It is useless talking to you; Regie, I'm waiting outside for you. Sota, anytime you need my help don't hesitate to come over to Abuja, I will still assist you for the sake of Aisosa and the children. Bye.

[Turns to leave]

Regie: Please, Nosa, wait a minute. We are about leaving now. Sota take this two hundred thousand naira; use it to solve the very pressing problems. This is all I can afford now. I am just trying to settle down in Abuja, thanks to Nosa.

Sota: That is okay. Please keep it on the table.

Regie: We must leave now. Sota, please try to come over to Abuja so we can all go over with you to apologise and ask Aisosa for forgiveness. That way you can both come back together again.

Sota: *[Jumps up]*

Will you get out of my house? What do you mean? Me? To go beg a woman to accept me back? God forbid, Regie what do you take me for, will you do that? A woman who was messing up with my closest friend in Abuja? Please if you have nothing good to say leave my house. Leave right away.

Regie: That's okay. Bye.

Nosa: Bye and take care of yourself.

[They both exit]

Sota: You can go to hell for all I care. Please keep out of my life.

[Returns to his seat]

I will rather die than accept assistance from Aisosa.

MOVEMENT 16

[Ede's house. Ede and Aisosa are dressed as if they have just returned from an outing. Headgears are seen resting on stools. They are relaxed on the settees.]

Ede: What an honour? A party just to celebrate your second term in office? That was wonderful. I really enjoyed myself; I wish we had stayed much longer.

Aisosa: I know, but we have to be at work tomorrow. More over, we promised your husband we wouldn't stay long. I don't know why they had to leave all of a sudden. I may as well sleep here tonight.

Ede: The house is all yours. Thank God for Cheryl, her husband and son were able to make it. When will they be leaving?

Aisosa: Tomorrow night.

Ede: Why so soon?

Aisosa: Past memories. She never even said a word about Rieme. It was only her husband who asked after her. As far as she is concerned Rieme is my child. That's the way she sees it. She shopped for all the children though.

Ede: Her husband is so humourous. He really loves her.

Aisosa: Yes, after that horrible marriage, God rewarded her with Peter.

Ede: Aisosa, congratulations once again. I am so happy for you. To become a Senate President a second time in Nigeria is a great achievement. This party by the President for you is well deserved.

Aisosa: Guess what, Ede?

Ede: Don't keep me in suspense, what is it?

Aisosa: The executive director for our National Research Institute whispered to me that our drug on HIV mother to child transmission has successfully scaled through all the tests at the Centre for Disease Control in Atlanta. The drug will be called Aisosaprin.

Ede: Fantastic. Congratulations!

         [Embracing her]

         After all those difficult clinical trials? Thank God you didn't give up.

Aisosa: This is my season of success.

Ede: Yes, indeed. This is sweet revenge. You know what Sosa, the best way to revenge when you have been thrown out, you are down and forgotten, is to succeed.

Aisosa: Yes, Ede, the best revenge is to succeed.

Ede: I hope Dr. Sota gets to hear of all these.

Aisosa: Who cares what he hears. He has too many problems to be bordered about who is succeeding and who is not. O what is the matter?

[Looking at her watch]

It's getting late and your husband is not here yet.

Ede: O relax, don't worry yourself *jo,* he is with Regie; we'll see him whenever we see him.

Aisosa: But he said we should not go to bed, that he has good news for us.

Ede: What other good news can be better than celebrating your second term as Senate President?

[Knock is heard]

Come in.

[Regie and Nosa enter with a bottle of Champaign in hand which they pop open as soon as they enter]

Nosa: Good news, good news, introducing to you the new minister of Petroleum Resources.

[Ede and Aisosa jump and embrace Regie]

Aisosa: *[Takes a bow]*

Congratulations, Your Excellency, sir. Where is your wife?

Nosa: She is on her way. The driver has gone to bring her

Ede: Congratulations, sir, for this well deserved honour.

Nosa: Now we are sure that Nigeria is on her path to change. Long Live Federal Republic of Nigeria.

Regie:	Someone is missing from here.
Nosa:	I know, Sota. What a shame!
Regie:	The last time I met him in Benin he was a sorry sight, leaving in someone's boy's quarters. What a pity. He said he will come to spend some time with me.
Aisosa:	Is he repentant now?
Regie:	Well not completely, but all that pride is gone. At least he shows appreciation when you give him some help.
Nosa:	He still refers to me as his wife snatcher though.
Aisosa:	Wife? Which wife? The wife he dumped? He should get a job. Regie, stop giving him money. Let him go and get himself a job.
Ede:	That is true. I think you should pressurise him to get a job before he looses his mind.
Aisosa:	That's okay let's go on with our celebration. Music please.
	[Music is on and they all start dancing]
Ede:	There is another good news...

[Light fades out]

MOVEMENT 17

[Aisosa's home. Sota is seated and served a soft drink; Aisosa walks in with her personal assistant carrying the files and portfolio behind her, obviously looking tired. As they enter Aisosa collects the things from her personal Assistant.]

Aisosa: Thanks, Abdul. Please try to make it here as early as 5.30am tomorrow. Ask my driver to take you home.

P.A: Thanks a lot, madam.

             [Exit]

Aisosa: You're welcome.

             [Turns to go in and notices Sota]

Aisosa: O Dr. Ojo, for God's sake what are you doing in my home?

Sota: Please, take it easy.

Aisosa: No, I won't. Are we in eternity so soon?

Sota: Forget about eternity. I hope you know the situation of things now.

Aisosa: No, I don't know.

Sota: Of course you do. After all you occupy my seat in the National Assembly now.

Aisosa: Oh! I didn't know you had your name engraved on a seat in the Senate. In any case I am the Senate President not the Chief Whip that you were. Moreover, I was returned unopposed two weeks ago. A second term in office.

Sota: Well, forget about that. I was only implying that I hope you are aware I am still unemployed.

Aisosa: Yes, I do. That is no news.

Sota: You know what it is like?

Aisosa: Of course I do. I was unemployed for eight years.

Sota: No it's not the same. After all you had a supportive husband by your side and a non-salary part-time work.

Aisosa: A part-time job, yes, a supportive husband by my side, no. What do you mean by that? Sota, you will never change. It's either you are suffering from partial amnesia or you are still your old, arrogant and unrepentant self.

Sota: Well, please don't let the past drive you against me.

Aisosa: Sometimes it is good for the past to drive you so long as it doesn't drive you crazy. Right now, you are about to drive me crazy.

Sota: Sorry about that. I am here to ask for a little favour from you.

[Make a move towards]

Aisosa: *[She stretches out her hand to curtail his move]*

You know what, Sota, add up your monthly expenses, multiply it by twelve and I will write a cheque for you to cover it, right away.

Sota: Thanks for your kind gesture. That's okay. I actually want more than your financial support for me. I would like to move in here to stay with you.

Aisosa: What? Move in here with me? Move into my house to become a husband of the senate president? A house I bought with my hard earned money. You, Sota Ojo? And you call this little favour? Little favour indeed. Is eternity so short? You have my house in Benin; go live in it.

[Sota goes on his knees and pleads with her]

Sota: Sorry Sosa, calm down. Don't get worked up unnecessarily over this simple issue. Well, I have come to realise that I was very unfair to you. You are a gracious woman Aisosa, a rare gem, a woman of virtue, please forgive me. I will make up for the past.

Aisosa: How? How would you do that Sota Ojo?

Sota: Please forget the bad moments, Aisosa. I am here for you now. I have come to stay for good.

Aisosa: Stay for good? Who told you I am interested in your stay? Sota, there is no need to plead. You see, let me make myself clear straight away, it won't work. When you left me I was an ugly, jobless, old, simple, fat, flabby bodied, a plain woman who had no name, no fame, no clothes, no money, no investment, without honour, but now, it is different. I am a world famous woman, rich, glamorous, gracious, elegant and an accomplished woman of rank. And to crown it all a two-time Senate President of the Federal Republic. I am a completely different Aisosa from the one you threw out on the street many years ago. That Aisosa is gone. This is a new Aisosa. A new Aisosa with a new image. So where do you fit in? How can you cope with this new me?

Sota: I will fit in. I can cope perfectly well. After all I am the man here, I was once a man of affluence, a man calibre too. I have learnt my lessons though. Together, we will make things work this time.

Aisosa: I have no place for you in my heart. I programmed you out of my mind long time ago. As you can see, things are different now. Well, get up and take a seat.

            [Motions him to a seat]

Sota: Thanks.

            [Still kneeling]

            Would you take me back? Would you accept me back as your lawful wedded husband? In poverty and sickness?

Aisosa: I am sorry, Sota, it won't work. I can see you haven't changed either. You are here out of necessity. I have my life well organised, it's not going to be easy to bring you in just like that. It will require a major reorganisation, which I am not prepared for. Go elsewhere, Sota, go get yourself another wife. Forget about me.

Sota: Aisosa, I have searched far and wide but there aren't Aisosa anywhere. It seems the manufacturers have stopped producing

Aisosas. They're off the shelves, they are out of stock.

Aisosa: What a pity? Sota, I am not even that Aisosa you once knew. Of a truth that Aisosa is obsolete. The manufacturer no longer produces them.

Sota: Please Aisosa, for the sake of our children give me another chance.

Aisosa: Which children? The children you threw out? Do you even know where they are right now? Sota, since you threw me out of your house a lot has happened. You do not expect me to bring you in just like that. If Cheryl were still around you wouldn't come here to plead. You are here because you have no alternative. What if I was on the street homeless and nameless would you have come seeking after me?

Sota: Please let's forget about Cheryl. Marrying her was a bad omen; it ruined my life. I live in Benin doing virtually nothing, leaving from hand to mouth. I tried to go back to Britain but the immigration there has blacklisted me.

[Aisosa laughs]

Aisosa: So this is your last and only bus stop?

Sota: Sincerely it is and please don't turn me away because I sold the house in Benin to pay up some debts. Sosa, if you don't take me in I will lose my sanity. I was carried away by the glamour and power of my new position then that I forgot those that really meant so much to me.

[Rises in an attempt to hold Aisosa, but Aisosa put forward her two hands]

Sosa darling, please forgive as you had always done. I will remain faithful to you forever.

Aisosa: I am not interested in your faithfulness. You see, Sota, our lives are a result of the choices we make in life, you have made your choice so learn to live with it.

Sota: Don't sound so unforgiving. Even God forgives us our sins when we ask for forgiveness.

Aisosa: Sota, I forgave you many years ago. The fact is that I do not want to go through the torture of marrying you a second time. I don't want to go through a failed marriage a second time. Sota, go back home think of what you can do to rise up again. Don't give me that responsibility. I won't do it for you.

Sota: You have no choice, Sosa, you are still my truly wedded wife, remember, this is our matrimonial home. Sosa, remember we used to be such a wonderful couple; we were called Sota and Sosa, the ideal couple. Many couples wanted to be like us. Those were wonderful days.

Aisosa: That is true. We had wonderful moments but you blew it all. Our lives together ended when you left for England several years ago. Sota, you know what? You can't put back the hand of the clock.

[Lights fade out]